Canada Close Up

Nunavut

Carrie Gleason

Scholastic Canada Ltd.

Toronto New York London Auckland Sydney
Mexico City New Delhi Hong Kong Buenos Aires

Visual Credits

Cover: Hans Blohm/Masterfile; p. i: Arctic-Images/SuperStock; p. iii: Gordon Wiltsie/National Geographic Stock; p. iv: (top) Fletcher & Baylis/Photo Researchers, Inc., (middle) iStockPhoto.com; p. 2: John Dunn/Arctic Light/National Geographic Stock; p. 3: Bryan & Cherry Alexander Photography/Alamy; p. 4: AirScapes/Paul Nopper; p. 6: (top) Paul Nicklen/National Geographic Stock, (bottom) Atlaspix/Shutterstock Inc.; p. 7: R Tanami/Ursus; p. 8: (top) Hemis/Alamy, (bottom) Ralph Roach/Shutterstock Inc.; p. 9: (top) Sideyman/Dreamstime.com, (bottom) iwka/Shutterstock Inc.; p. 10: (middle) Vinicius Tupinamba/Shutterstock Inc., (bottom) Nick Norman/National Geographic Stock; p. 11: Rob Howard/Corbis; p. 12: Galen Rowell/Mountain Light/Alamy; p. 13: tbkmedia.de/Alamy; p. 14: Interfoto/Alamy; p. 15: Tamara Kulikova/Shutterstock Inc.; p. 16: The London Art Archive/Alamy; p. 17: Wolfgang Kaehler/Alamy; p. 18: Hulton-Deutsch Collection/Corbis; p. 19: R Tanami/Ursus; p. 20: Margaret Bourke-White/Time Life Pictures/Getty Images; p. 21: D.B. Marsh/Library and Archives Canada/e007914440; p. 23: Carlo Allegri/AFP/Getty Images; p. 24: (top) B&C Alexander/First Light, (bottom) Wolfgang Kaehler/Alamy; p. 25: Library and Archives Canada, Acc. No. R9266-2127 Peter Winkworth Collection of Canadiana; p. 26: Yvette Cardozo/Maxx Images; p. 27: Brian Summers/First Light; p. 28: Ron Haufman; p. 29: (top) John Foster/Masterfile, (bottom) Bryan & Cherry Alexander/Photo Researchers, Inc; p. 30: (top) Vladimir Melnik/Shutterstock Inc., (bottom) B&C Alexander/First Light; p. 31: (top) Tischenko Irina/Shutterstock Inc., (bottom) B&C Alexander/First Light; p. 32: Yvette Cardozo/Maxx Images; p. 33: (top) Eleonora Kolomiyets/Shutterstock Inc., (bottom) CP PHOTO/Jeff McIntosh; p. 34: (top) Danita Delimont/Alamy, (bottom) Bryan & Cherry Alexander Photography/Alamy; p. 35: Michael Melford/National Geographic Stock; p. 36: B&C Alexander/First Light; p. 37: Bryan & Cherry Alexander Photography/Alamy; p. 38: B&C Alexander/First Light; p. 39: B&C Alexander/First Light; p. 40: Staffan Widstrand/Corbis; p. 41: AP Photo/Fort McMurray Today/Carl Patzel; p. 42: CP Photo/Nathan Denette; p. 43: (top) Courtesy Everett collection/CP Photos, (bottom) Judith Eglington/Judith Eglington fonds/PA-140297 Reproduced with the permission of Library and Archives Canada; back cover © 2009 Jupiterimages Corporation.

Produced by Plan B Book Packagers
Editorial: Ellen Rodger
Design: Rosie Gowsell-Pattison
Special thanks to consultant and editor Terrance Cox, adjunct professor, Brock University;
Adrianna Morganelli, Tanya Rutledge, Jim Chernishenko

Library and Archives Canada Cataloguing in Publication

Gleason, Carrie, 1973-
Nunavut / Carrie Gleason.
(Canada close up)
Includes index.
ISBN 978-0-545-98912-1

1. Nunavut--Juvenile literature. I. Title. II. Series: Canada
close up (Toronto, Ont.)

FC4311.2.G54 2009   j971.9'5   C2009-901199-9

ISBN-10 0-545-98912-4

6 5 4 3 2 1   Printed in Canada   09 10 11 12 13 14

Contents

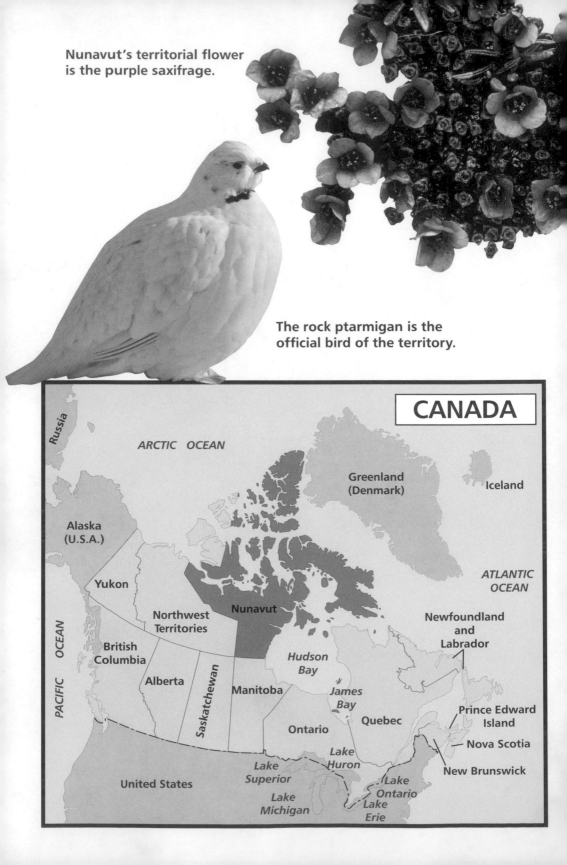

Nunavut's territorial flower is the purple saxifrage.

The rock ptarmigan is the official bird of the territory.

CANADA

Russia

ARCTIC OCEAN

Greenland (Denmark)

Iceland

Alaska (U.S.A.)

Yukon

ATLANTIC OCEAN

Northwest Territories

Nunavut

Newfoundland and Labrador

PACIFIC OCEAN

British Columbia

Alberta

Saskatchewan

Manitoba

Hudson Bay

James Bay

Quebec

Prince Edward Island

Nova Scotia

Ontario

New Brunswick

Lake Huron

Lake Superior

Lake Ontario

United States

Lake Michigan

Lake Erie

Welcome to Nunavut!

Welcome to Canada's newest territory! Nunavut was created on April 1, 1999. It is home to the Inuit peoples of the Far North. In their language, Inuktitut, Nunavut means "our land."

"Our land" is the barren tundra and eastern islands of the Canadian Arctic. It takes special skills and knowledge to live in this cold environment. The territory has a population of just over 31,000 and most residents are Inuit. Their ancestors knew the ways of the land and left messages in piles of rocks called *inuksuit*, which have become symbols of the north.

Modern life here is a mix of old ways and new. Today most Inuit live in small permanent communities, not "out on the land" like their ancestors. They still depend on the animals of the land and sea. Read on to find out why Nunavut's motto is "our land, our strength."

1

Chapter 1
North of 60

People who live in Nunavut are called Nunavummiut. Living "north of 60" refers to the fact that most of Nunavut lies north of 60 degrees latitude. The territory is made up of two main parts: the Arctic mainland and the eastern Arctic islands.

Snowmobiles are as common as cars in Qikiqtarjuaq, an island community on the east coast of Baffin Island.

The Arctic Archipelago

An archipelago is a group of islands. The Arctic Archipelago is one of the world's largest. It is made up of thousands of Arctic Ocean islands of varying sizes. Most belong to Nunavut. The rest are part of the Northwest Territories, Nunavut's neighbour to the west. Some, such as Victoria Island and Melville Island, are shared between the two.

Baffin Island is Nunavut's – and Canada's – largest island. It is also the site of Iqaluit, the territory's capital city. Ellesmere is the northernmost island. Others include the Queen Elizabeth Island group, Devon Island and Axel Heiberg Island. Nunavut also includes all the islands in Hudson and James bays!

A **glacier** winds through Akshayuk Pass in Baffin Island's Auyuittuq National Park.

Mountains and ice

The Arctic Cordillera is a series of mountain ranges that stretches from northern Ellesmere Island along the east coast of Baffin Island. These are among Canada's highest mountains, and the only major mountains in the east.

In the mountains farthest north, the average summer temperature is only –2 degrees Celsius. Some mountains are permanently covered by ice caps, such as the Agassiz Ice Cap on the northern coast of Ellesmere Island. Ice caps are large sheets of ice left over from the last **ice age**. Some are found farther south too. The Barnes Ice Cap on Baffin Island is Canada's oldest. It is more than 18,000 years old!

Other mountains are bare rock or glacier-covered. A glacier is different from an ice cap in that it moves in only one direction and usually lies in a valley, whereas an ice cap flows in all directions. Bylot Island, off the north coast of Baffin Island, is almost completely covered by glaciers. Thousands of glaciers can be found throughout the Arctic islands.

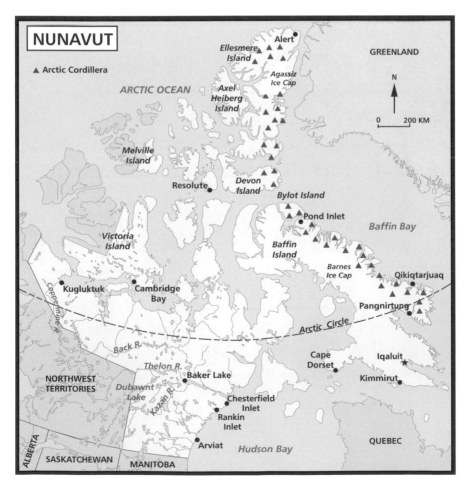

Narwhals, clustered here in an Arctic island channel, live year-round in the Arctic. So do bowhead and beluga whales. In summer they are joined by migrating killer, blue and sperm whales.

Lowland islands

Most of the Arctic islands are flat and rocky, broken up by low hills and long gravel ridges. The islands in the northwest make up one of the driest regions in Canada. This area is called a polar desert. Here, **precipitation** rarely falls, and the low temperature means that it is too cold for the existing ice to melt.

Many channels and passageways run between the islands. When the water freezes over in winter, it forms one giant world of ice.

Seals and walruses swim in these frigid waters. Ringed seals are a main source of food for the polar bears that are found throughout the Arctic, both on land and in water.

The Arctic mainland

The Arctic mainland and Baffin Island are part of the Canadian Shield, a landform that covers most of eastern Canada. It was formed billions of years ago and contains some of the oldest, most mineral-rich rock in the world.

The land got its shape as glaciers moved over it during the last ice age, carving out many lakes and rivers. The largest mainland lake is Dubawnt Lake. Rivers such as the Back and Coppermine flow into the Arctic, while the Thelon and Kazan rivers empty into Hudson Bay. There are so many smaller lakes and rivers here that some have not even been named.

The Tree River winds through the mainland to the Arctic Ocean.

On Axel Heiberg Island in the Far North, the fossilized remains of trees have been found. This suggests that 45 million years ago this Arctic island was warm enough to support a lush forest!

The southernmost part of the Nunavut mainland is forested. Spruce, poplar, aspen and birch trees grow here. Moose, beaver, muskrat, fox, timber wolf and black bear live in these forests. Moving north, the trees get smaller, the forests thin out and tundra dominates the landscape. The zone where this change happens is called the treeline.

Timber wolves roam Nunavut's southern forests.

Tundra and permafrost

Most of Nunavut is covered in tundra. Tundra is an area of barren, frozen ground. Trees cannot grow here because their roots cannot penetrate into the permafrost – the layer of frozen soil below the surface. Usually, the top layer of soil thaws in summer. This allows plants such as dwarf birches, **lichens** and mosses to grow. These plants spread their branches along the ground to protect them from the harsh winds. Berries such as crowberries, blueberries, alpine bearberries and cranberries grow, even though the ground is frozen.

Huge herds of barren-ground caribou migrate across the tundra, eating lichen. Peary caribou live on the Arctic islands. Woolly muskoxen feed on grasses around lakes and in meadows during summer.

Cranberries grow in tundra bogs.

A land of winter

Nunavut is the coldest place in Canada. Winter lasts for nine months of the year. The east coasts of Baffin and Ellesmere islands get the highest snowfall. But most of the territory receives very little precipitation. Temperatures in winter often drop below −30 degrees Celsius.

Summers are short, lasting for about two months. Temperatures rise to an average of 9 degrees Celsius, causing the snow and ice to melt. Where snow melts, wetlands form. The water sits on the surface because it cannot seep down through the frozen soil of the permafrost underneath. This creates an ideal environment for billions of mosquitoes and blackflies. These swarms of insects provide food for millions of **migratory** birds that come to the wetlands to breed each summer.

In summer, Nunavut is bathed in light – even at night! This has given the Arctic the name "land of the midnight sun." At the height of winter, darkness lasts 24 hours a day.

Nunavut facts

- Nunavut is the largest of all the provinces and territories. It covers an area of 2,093,190 square kilometres. This is over 21 per cent of Canada's total area.

- Barbeau Peak, on Ellesmere Island, is Nunavut's highest point at 2616 metres.

- Nettilling Lake, on Baffin Island, is the territory's largest freshwater lake. It is frozen over with ice for most of the year.

Chapter 2
Becoming Nunavut

About 85 per cent of the people living in Nunavut today are Inuit. Inuit means "the people." The ancestors of the Inuit, and the people who came before them, were the first to learn the hunting, trapping and winter survival skills of the Arctic way of life.

The rest are *qallunaat*, or non–Inuit, who have come from the south to work here.

The first peoples

People from Siberia migrated across the northern coasts of Alaska and settled in what is now Nunavut about 4000 years ago. The Inuit call these people *Sivullirmiut*, or first people. They used stone weapons to hunt caribou, seals and walruses.

Arctic warming

The Arctic had periods of freezing and thawing, which brought new peoples to the area, among them the Dorsets, whom the Inuit call *Tuuniit*, meaning "the giants." During a period of warming, around 1000 A.D., people called the Thule moved from Alaska to Nunavut. They came with boats made of sealskin, from which they hunted whales and other large sea animals. On land they had dogs to pull their winter sleds. They built snow houses, as the people of the Dorset culture had done before them.

For most of the year, the Thule lived along the coasts in small villages. When another Arctic cooling period began in the 1600s and whales became scarce, they hunted seals and walruses and moved inland to hunt caribou. This change in lifestyle marks the beginning of the Inuit culture.

Reconstruction of a Thule summer house near Resolute

The Vikings

About the same time that the Thule came from the west, the Vikings arrived from the east. Originally from Scandinavia, the Vikings had sailed to Greenland and set up a **colony** there in 985 A.D. Viking sagas, or stories, tell about the land they discovered and named *Helluland*, or "land of flat stones." Today this land is called Baffin Island.

The Northwest Passage

Over 500 years after the Vikings, Europeans made their second appearance in the Arctic. This time, they were explorers from England, looking for a water route to the Pacific called the Northwest Passage.

Martin Frobisher

In 1576 British explorer Martin Frobisher landed at Iqaluit, on Baffin Island. After a fight between five of his crew and the Inuit there, Frobisher kidnapped an Inuk man and returned with him to England, where the man died.

Frobisher returned to the Arctic the following year to look for gold. There, he collected 200 tonnes of rock and returned to England with an Inuit family: a father, mother and child. All of them died from diseases against which they had no **immunity**. And what Frobisher had discovered was not gold, but a metal called iron pyrite, also known as "fool's gold."

More attempts

Frobisher's voyage led many to believe that a passageway could be found through the Arctic. John Davis made three voyages to Arctic waters, beginning in 1585, and mapped part of the Baffin Island coast. In the early 1600s Henry Hudson sailed south of Baffin Island and discovered what is now Hudson Bay. When his crew stopped to trade with the Inuit near Digges Island, a fight broke out and some of the English sailors were killed.

Other explorers, such as William Baffin and Robert Bylot, followed Hudson's voyages, but they determined that the Arctic ice made passage impossible.

Across the Arctic

Two centuries later, John Franklin mapped two-thirds of Canada's Arctic coast. In 1845 he returned with two ships, *Terror* and *Erebus*, to find the Northwest Passage. Late in 1846 the ships became trapped in ice. Many rescue expeditions failed to find them, but did discover that Franklin died in June 1847 and that, by the spring of 1848, a total of 24 men were dead. The remaining 105 men then left the ships to trek south on foot. No one survived. Some frozen remains suggest that they died of starvation, scurvy or lead poisoning from their tinned food.

Finally, in 1906, Norwegian explorer Roald Amundsen succeeded in reaching the Pacific Ocean by ship.

The Franklin expedition

Inuit hunters traditionally used kayaks and harpoons to hunt seals, birds and caribou.

Whaling

In the early 1800s Europeans and Americans discovered the wealth of whales that lived in the Arctic waters. This launched a whaling industry that would last about 100 years – until the whales were hunted nearly out of existence.

The baleen, or bone, from bowhead whales was used to make women's **corsets** and buggy whips. The blubber, or fat, was boiled down to make soap, paint and fuel for lamps.

When the bowhead whales began to decline, the whalers turned to killing belugas and narwhals, until they too became scarce.

Fox pelts hang outside of a fur trading post.

Arctic ownership

Since 1670 southern Nunavut had been part of Rupert's Land, a vast area belonging to the fur trading Hudson's Bay Company. At fur trading posts, Aboriginal and European trappers traded animal pelts, such as beaver and mink, for blankets and metal tools.

The areas west of Rupert's Land were referred to as the North-Western Territory, and included the Arctic islands and most of the Arctic mainland. In 1870 the lands of the fur trading companies passed into the hands of the recently formed Canadian government. All of Nunavut became part of the Northwest Territories, except the High Arctic, which Britain passed on to Canada in 1880.

Bloody Falls

Explorers working in the fur trade also tried to find the Northwest Passage. In 1771 Samuel Hearne became the first European to reach the Arctic Ocean overland. He travelled with **Dene** guides from Manitoba northward through the Northwest Territories and Nunavut, and along the Coppermine River to its end at the Arctic Ocean. Fifteen kilometres from their destination, the Dene, traditional enemies of the Inuit, **massacred** an encampment of local Inuit. Hearne named the site of the massacre Bloody Falls.

Bloody Falls is a set of rapids near the mouth of the Coppermine River. Today, it is part of Kugluk Territorial Park and is a national historic site.

Arctic trading posts

About the time Arctic whaling ended, Arctic fox pelts became popular. This provided the Inuit with a new item to trade. The Hudson's Bay Company set up trading posts in the Arctic in the early 1900s for Arctic fox and polar bear furs, seal and walrus skins and narwhal tusks.

The company encouraged the Inuit to trade these items in return for guns and metal tools, cotton cloth, flour, tea and sugar. Other fur trading companies also set up posts.

An Inuit hunter trades animal pelts for goods shipped from the south in this 1937 photograph.

Mission schools, like the Anglican Church Mission School at Arviat, were run by missionaries from the south.

To gain control of the area, the Canadian government sent the Royal Canadian Mounted Police to the Arctic in 1903. They went to trading posts and Inuit camps to inform the people that they lived in Canada.

Changing lives

First whalers, then fur traders, brought big changes to the way the Inuit lived. They no longer lived solely off the land as their ancestors did. They now depended on a system of trade.

Missionaries who had come to the Arctic with whalers and fur traders became friendly with the Inuit. They converted many to Christianity and convinced many to give up their old beliefs. They also set up schools and medical centres.

War and work

During **World War II,** an American military base was built at Iqaluit. Local Inuit were hired to build an airstrip from which military supplies would be flown to Europe, where the fighting took place.

By the time the war ended, the U.S. and Canada were enemies with the Soviet Union. Fearing an attack, they set up a system of **radar** sites and airfields across the Arctic, from Baffin Island to Alaska. This was called the Distant Early Warning (DEW) line. Many Inuit gave up trapping and hunting and turned to jobs there instead. The jobs came and went. A nickel mine opened in Rankin Inlet and Inuit settled nearby to work there. But, by 1962, it had closed and many Inuit were out of work again.

Government action

In the 1950s the Canadian government tried to change the lives of the Inuit. They built houses, schools and hospitals, encouraging all Inuit to abandon life on the land.

In the 1960s, **co-ops** were started to sell Inuit arts and crafts in the south. After oil was discovered in Alaska, exploration in the Canadian Arctic began too. Inuit **activists** began to talk about their rights to the land and the loss of their traditions. They pressured the Canadian government to acknowledge their right to the land and its **resources**.

A new territory

In 1982 people in the Northwest Territories voted for an Inuit territory in the east. On July 9, 1993, a **land claim** agreement was signed with the Canadian government. It is celebrated each year as Nunavut Day.

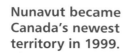

Nunavut became Canada's newest territory in 1999.

Chapter 3
The Hunt

Traditionally, every part of a hunted animal was used by the Inuit. Skins were used for clothing and tents. Animal blubber, or fat, was burned as heating or cooking oil. Bones and ivory tusks were used to make tools.

Sealskin is still used today as a tent covering at Inuit summer hunting camps, like this one at Cape Dorset, Baffin Island. An *ulu* (right) is a traditional tool used to scrape animal hides.

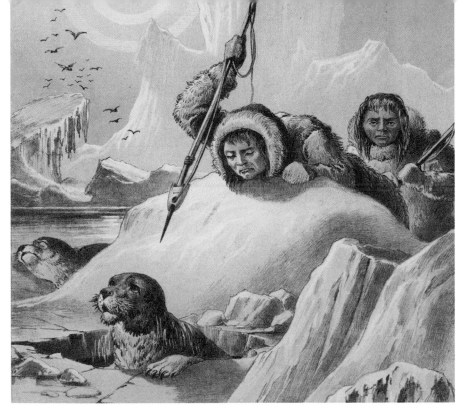

Seal hunters used harpoons made from driftwood and animal bones.

The seal hunt

Seals have always been one of the most important animals to the Inuit. They are hunted year-round.

Traditionally, hunters waited at breathing holes in the ice to harpoon seals that came up for air. On open water, they would use a harpoon with an attached float made from a bladder or sealskin, to prevent the harpooned seal from diving. Today hunters use rifles as well as wood and metal harpoons.

Winter homes

Traditional winter homes were snow houses called *igluit*, or igloos. They were made of blocks carved from hard snow. Some had two rooms, one where the family lived and the other where they stored meat and supplies.

Through the long Arctic winters, the Inuit spent a lot of time together indoors, playing games and telling stories. During the day, seal-oil lamps and body heat would melt the inside walls. At night, when the lamps were out and everyone had crawled into caribou sleeping bags, the walls would freeze again. This constant thawing and refreezing made the igloo walls stronger.

Inuksuit

The Arctic tundra has often been called the Barren Lands. There are very few geographic markers here. To give direction or communicate information about a place to hunt, the Inuit built *inuksuit*. These large stone piles still dominate the Arctic landscape. Some were built as memorials to people who died nearby.

Caribou migrate each year to and from their calving grounds. This herd is travelling through the Meliadine River Valley near Rankin Inlet.

The caribou hunt

In spring, summer and fall, the Inuit lived in tents covered with animal skins. Muskoxen and caribou were hunted in the summer.

To hunt caribou, *inuksuit* in the shape of humans were built. Called *inunnguat,* these stone towers, built on the side of a lake or river on the caribou's migration path, worked to divert the caribou into the water. Caribou are much slower in water than they are on land, and made easier targets for hunters in kayaks. Caribou were also corralled into tight spots using stone walls that hunters hid behind.

The Inuit built two kinds of boats for sea travel. Kayaks were narrow, one-person boats. The larger *umiaks* were used for carrying people and supplies from camp to camp or for hunting whales.

Fishing

In summer, fish were caught in streams and rivers using weirs. Weirs are stone fences that divert fish to shallow waters where they are easier to catch with spears. The fishing spear, called a *kakivak*, was made by attaching three prongs of caribou antler to a pole. The outside prongs held the fish while the middle one pierced it.

A man uses a spear to fish for Arctic char.

Chapter 4
Arctic Living

Hunting caribou, seal and fish today is estimated to be worth $30 million to $50 million to the Nunavut economy. But this money doesn't come from selling the meat or skins. It's the amount of money it would cost the Inuit to replace this traditional food source with food and goods from the south!

Wild foods, such as seal, are much cheaper than foods that need to be shipped in.

A hunter hangs fillets of Arctic char to dry at an Inuit summer fishing camp.

Transportation costs

Nunavut is very remote, or far away, from almost everywhere else. The land here is too cold and dry for crops to grow. Everything that is sold in stores is brought in, either on planes or boats. These transportation costs increase the prices of store-bought goods in Nunavut to three or four times more than in the rest of Canada. A jug of orange juice costs more than $10!

Inuit women buy food shipped from the south at a grocery store in Baker Lake.

Tourists wearing sealskin boots and coats rest on a sled. Tourism is an important source of income in the north.

Working

Many Nunavummiut work in the service industry. The government is the biggest employer. People work as politicians, police officers, teachers, nurses and doctors.

The majority of Nunavummiut work for wages only part of the year, in fishing, construction and hunting. Some hunters and fishers sell their meat locally.

Tourism is another service industry where people find seasonal work. Tour operators run hunting and fishing lodges or take visitors out on the land. Tourism also creates jobs in restaurants and hotels.

Mining

Billions of dollars worth of minerals lie beneath Nunavut. Lead, zinc, gold, uranium and diamonds have all been mined here.

Jobs in mining come and go quickly. One of the first mines in Nunavut was a mica mine in Kimmirut, which operated from 1900 until 1913. Inuit and Scottish miners worked there. The Polaris zinc and lead mine, on Cornwallis Island near Resolute, opened in 1980 and closed in 2002. It was the most northerly metal mine in the world. In 2006 the Jericho Diamond Mine opened, but closed in 2008. The mines try to hire as many northerners as possible.

Heavy equipment digs into the soil at the Jericho Diamond Mine. Nunavut's first diamond mine closed two years after it opened.

Arts and crafts

Almost one-half of Inuit households today make money by creating arts and crafts. These are usually made in the home and then passed on to a co-op, which sells the items to collectors and galleries in the south.

The earliest Inuit art works were carvings made out of soft materials such as whalebone, antler and ivory. **Soapstone** was also used because it was a soft material for carving. The carvings were of hunting scenes, people or animals.

Using modern metal tools, Inuit craftspeople now make their carvings out of harder materials such as serpentine, basalt, marble or quartz, depending on what is at hand.

Art prints that show scenes from Arctic life or legends are also sold to southern galleries.

The fishing industry

Arctic char is the most northerly freshwater fish in the world, found as far north as Ellesmere Island. It is caught by fishers and taken to processing plants in Cambridge Bay, Rankin Inlet, Pangnirtung or Iqaluit. There it is skinned and frozen. Daily flights out of Nunavut deliver the fish to markets throughout North America. Other important offshore fisheries in Nunavut catch shrimp and turbot. Shrimp are frozen and flown to Europe and Japan.

Arctic char has been an important part of the Inuit diet for thousands of years.

Oil and gas

Nunavut has almost one-quarter of Canada's natural gas reserves, and about ten per cent of its oil. Nunavut's climate makes extracting these resources difficult. Special equipment is needed to drill through the frozen ground and, for offshore drilling, to withstand the force of crushing sea ice. Sea ice also creates a problem for shipping **fossil fuels**. The biggest fuel reserves are in the Sverdrup Basin, just west of Axel Heiberg Island.

Chapter 5
Inuit Culture Today

Today, most Inuit live in one of the territory's 26 communities. The communities are located far away from one another and, except for Baker Lake, are on the coasts. Each has a landing strip and a harbour. The largest are Iqaluit, Rankin Inlet and Arviat.

Getting around

There are few roads in Nunavut. Most people drive all-terrain vehicles. In winter, people drive on top of the snow in snowmobiles or trucks. To get from one community to another, people take regularly scheduled flights or they **charter** a plane.

All buildings in Nunavut sit completely above ground. Even pipes for water and fuel and hydro wires are above ground.

Mush, mush!

The Canadian Inuit dog is the official animal of Nunavut. Teams of dogs pull a sled called a *qamutiik*. Traditionally the sleds were made from driftwood, animal bones and ivory. Snowmobiles have today mostly taken the place of dogsleds, but many people still use them for sport. Others keep sled dogs as pets.

Language and learning

Nunavut has three official languages: French, English and Inuktitut. Inuktitut is the everyday spoken language. Some classes in schools are taught in Inuktitut and it is broadcast over the radio. Inuktitut is written using symbols that represent syllables.

Some school breaks are planned around the spring and fall hunting seasons. Elders are invited into the classrooms to teach children the old ways. Inuit *Qaujimajatuqangit* means "traditional knowledge." It teaches people how to be members of a community and to work together, to use resources at hand to solve problems, and to live off and respect the land. These principles are based on the traditional Inuit way of life.

Country food

Traditional Inuit food is called "country food." This includes caribou, whale, seal, walrus, duck, Arctic char and berries. The Inuit share the meat they hunt and catch with others. In larger communities such as Iqaluit, people can buy country food. There are even country food snacks, such as *muktaaq*, pieces of raw whale skin with a thin layer of fat. Caribou jerky is tough, dried meat. One traditional treat, called Inuit ice cream, is not like any other ice cream. It includes melted caribou fat, meat and salt, and is cooked and then frozen before eating.

Muktaaq is raw and can be eaten fresh or frozen.

Arctic sports

Traditional Inuit sports are usually an individual challenge or played between two people, and require little equipment. Many are feats of strength that at one time were useful for survival. The hand pull, arm pull and one-hand reach all require strength and control. High kicking involves jumping eight to nine feet into the air to touch a marker suspended above. Other Inuit games have names like the seal hop and the muskox wrestle. Athletes perform these events at the annual Northern Games or the Arctic Winter Games.

A Nunavut athlete stretches to hit a small seal dummy in the Alaskan high kick competition at the Arctic Winter Games.

Chapter 6
Points of Pride

▶ The military base at Alert, on the tip of Ellesmere Island, is the northernmost permanent settlement in the world. It was built as a weather station in the 1950s. In 2006 there were five people living there.

▶ Singer Tanya Tagaq Gillis from Cambridge Bay is known throughout the world for her throat singing — rhythmic sound patterns traditionally performed by two women as a vocal game.

▶ Baker Lake is the geographic centre of Canada.

▶ Susan Aglukark is a famous singer and songwriter from Arviat. She uses both English words and Inuktitut chants in her songs.

▶ Peter Pitseolak was a famous photographer who took over 2000 pictures of Inuit life. Over a period of twenty years, he documented a changing way of life in the north.

▶ Cape Dorset is known as the Inuit art capital. Artists in this community of just over 1200 near the southern tip of Baffin Island have produced almost 50,000 art prints depicting Inuit life. Artist Kenojuak Ashevak's work has appeared on a Canadian stamp and a Canadian quarter.

Glossary

activists: People who campaign to bring about social or political change

charter: To reserve an aircraft for a special flight

colony: A new settlement controlled by another country

co-ops: Businesses owned and run jointly by their members

corsets: Tightly fitted women's undergarments to shape women's torsos

Dene: Aboriginal peoples of northern Canada who speak an Athapaskan language

fossil fuels: Fuels made from coal, oil or natural gas. They are formed from the remains of plants and animals that lived long ago

glaciers: Masses of slow-moving, compacted snow and ice

ice age: A period of history when most of Earth was covered in ice

immunity: Resistance to a disease or infection

land claim: A legal declaration of desired control over an area

lichens: Slow-growing plants that are a combination of a fungus and algae

massacred: Killed in large numbers

migratory: Describes an animal that changes where it lives with the seasons

missionaries: Members of a religious group sent to spread their faith

precipitation: Rain, snow or sleet

radar: An electromagnetic system for detecting the presence of something or its distance

resources: Reserves of minerals, fossil fuels, trees and animals in a geographic area

soapstone: A soft rock that can be easily carved

World War II: An international conflict (1939-1945) that spread throughout Europe, North Africa, southeast Asia and the western Pacific, and claimed an estimated 55 million lives